Robots in Space

Nancy Furstinger

Lerner Publications Company
Minneapolis

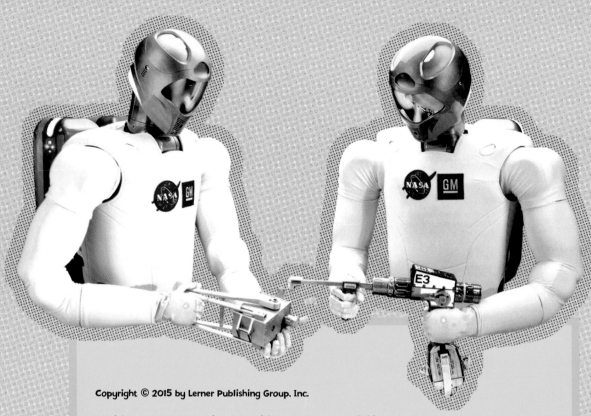

Lerner Publications Company
A division of Lerner Publishing Group, Inc.
241 First Avenue North
Minneapolis, MN 55401 USA

For reading levels and more information, look up this title at www.lernerbooks.com.

Cover photo: Curiosity, a robot that NASA launched in 2011, is still gathering information as it travels the surface of Mars.

Library of Congress Cataloging-in-Publication Data

Furstinger, Nancy, author.
Robots in space — by Nancy Furstinger.
    pages   cm. — (Lightning bolt books™ — Robots everywhere!)
Includes index.
ISBN 978-1-4677-4055-5 (lib. bdg. : alk. paper)
ISBN 978-1-4677-4692-2 (eBook)
    1. Space robotics—Juvenile literature. 2. Robots—Juvenile literature. 3. Space probes—Juvenile literature. 4. Outer space—Exploration—Juvenile literature. I. Title.
TL1097.F87 2015
629.43—dc23   2013046118

Manufactured in the United States of America
1 — BP — 7/15/14

Table of Contents

What is a Robot?

Robots are machines that can move around and do work. They carry out commands.

Many robots team up with people to complete jobs.

This space robot uses a camera to see the planet below.

Scientists design robots to
solve problems. Scientists
think about what tools and
skills robots need. Then the
scientists build the best
robots for the job.

Scientists use strong metals and plastics to build robots. Tough robots can work in space. Extreme heat and cold do not stop them.

Scientists test space robots on Earth.

Some space robots look like you. They have hands to grab tools. Others look like cars. They drive across planets.

Scientists send commands using radio signals. They tell space robots how to use their sensors. They also tell the robots how to move.

Huge antennas send commands to robots in space.

Space Probes

Probes are robots that explore space. They travel to other planets. Scientists guide probes from Earth.

Probes travel to space on rockets.

Probes study our solar system. Some land on planets. Others fly around planets.

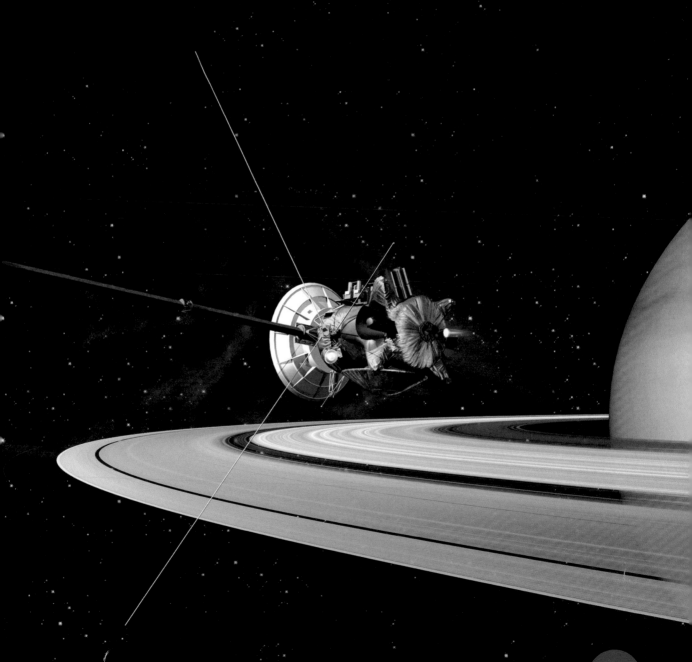

Probes take in lots of data. They send it back to Earth by radio. But most probes never return to Earth.

Probes use antennas to send data to Earth.

Probes have explored Saturn and Jupiter. One probe landed on Saturn's moon Titan. Another found rings around Jupiter.

The probe that went to Titan used a parachute to slow down when it landed.

One probe landed on Venus. This planet is very hot. It is too hot for people to explore.

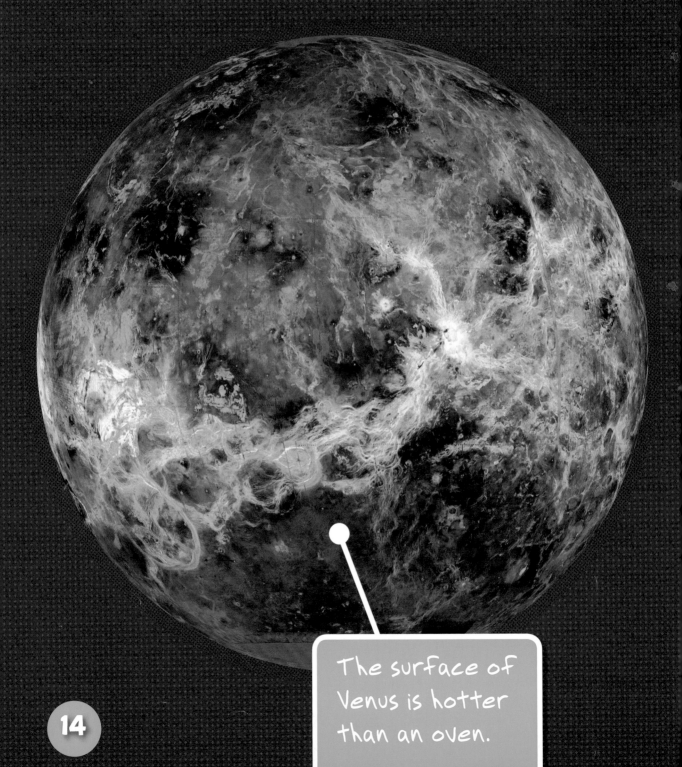

The surface of Venus is hotter than an oven.

Another probe has flown very far. It left Earth in 1977. Now it is 12 billion miles (19 billion kilometers) from the Sun. It helps scientists learn what is outside our solar system.

Helping Humans in Space

Some space robots have parts that look like human heads and arms. Astronauts use these robots to do hard jobs.

Scientists work side by side with robots in space.

Space robots work at the International Space Station. One looks like the top half of a person. Scientists control its arms and fingers.

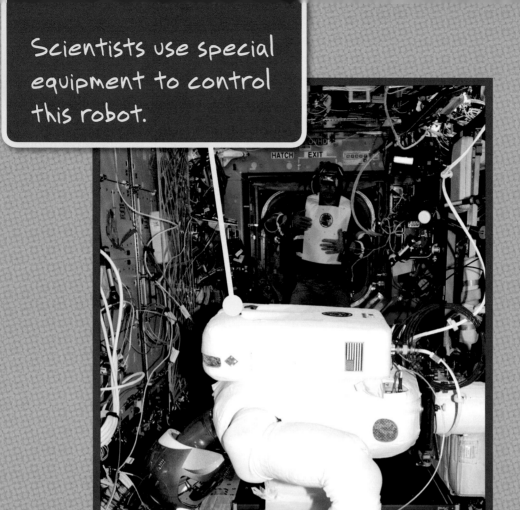

Scientists use special equipment to control this robot.

The human-shaped robot stays inside the space station. It helps the crew use tools. It fixes objects in the station.

Scientists plan to give the robot legs. Then it will be able to go outside. It will check the space station for damage. It will help make repairs.

The International Space Station is huge. Having a robot helper will be useful to the crew.

Other types of robots work outside the space station. One has arms to hold tools. Its arms are 11 feet (3.4 meters) long.

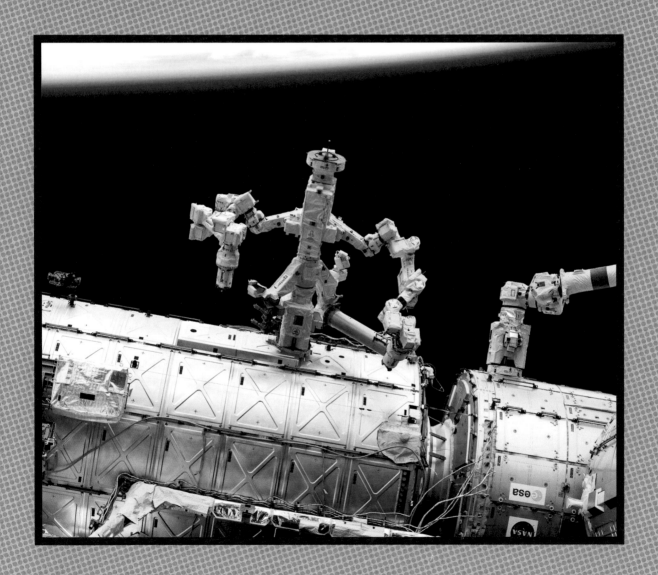

This robot gets help moving around. It rides at the end of a 56-foot (17 m) robotic arm. This lets it work on different parts of the station.

This robot helps attach new parts to the space station.

Rovers are space robots with wheels. Some are as small as a skateboard. Others are as big as a car.

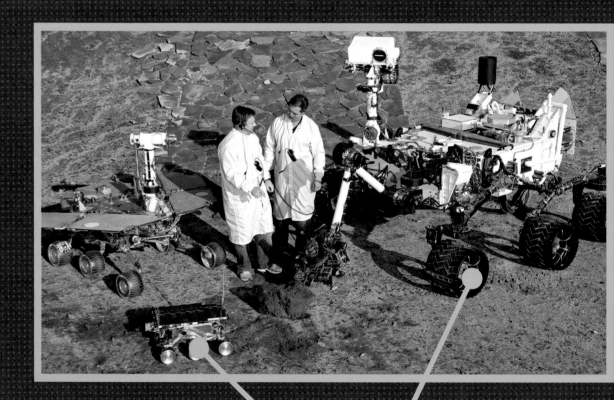

Rovers come in different sizes.

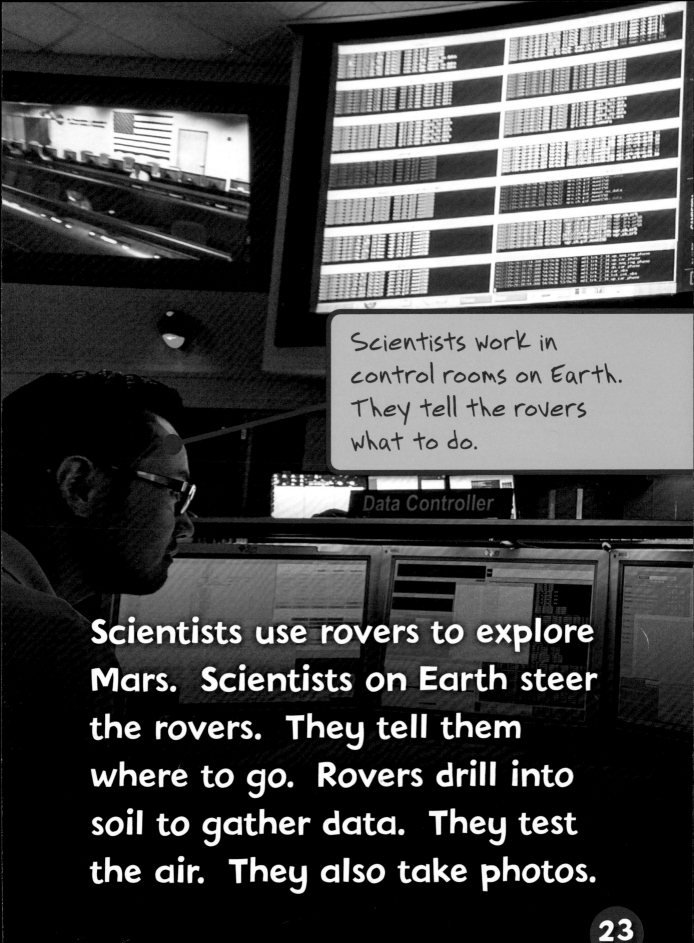

Scientists work in control rooms on Earth. They tell the rovers what to do.

Data Controller

Scientists use rovers to explore Mars. Scientists on Earth steer the rovers. They tell them where to go. Rovers drill into soil to gather data. They test the air. They also take photos.

New rovers carry tiny science labs. They fire lasers at rocks. Sensors measure the light that bounces back. Scientists can use this data to learn what is inside the rocks.

Looking at rocks and dirt can tell scientists if water is present.

One rover made a special discovery in September 2013. It found water in Mars's soil. Scientists think this means Mars may have once had life. But no signs of life have been found yet.

So far, only robots have been to Mars.

But scientists plan to send people there by 2035.

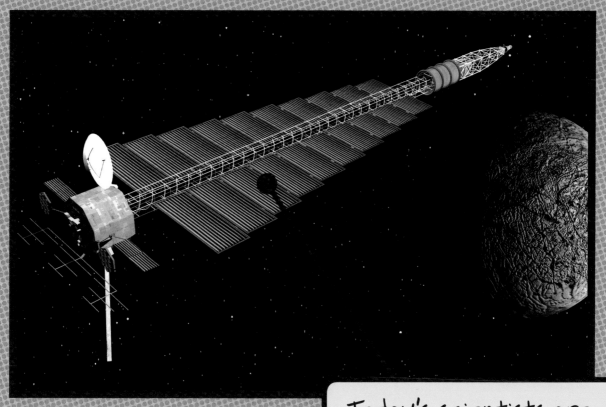

Today's scientists are imagining the space robots of the future.

Scientists will keep making space robots. New robots will go farther. They will do more jobs. They will help us learn more about our solar system.

Robot Scientists

- You need good grades in math and science to become a space robot scientist. You will also need to study astronomy, engineering, and computer science.

- Some scientists design probes in labs. Other scientists travel to the International Space Station to work with robots there.

- Scientists test robots before sending them into space. They use special machines to shake the robots. They make sure the robots will launch and land without breaking.

Fun Facts

- One space probe carries pictures and sounds from Earth. Scientists sent the pictures and sounds in case aliens find the probe someday. The aliens could see and hear what Earth is like. The probe also has directions to Earth.

- The human-shaped robot on the International Space Station is strong. But it can also be used for delicate jobs. Its fingers are so gentle they can pick up paper without crinkling it.

- The world's first talking robot soared into space in 2013. Japanese scientists built it. The robot takes photos and speaks to astronauts.

- The United States sent a pair of rovers to Mars in 2003. They were designed to work for ninety days. But one of them worked for more than ten years!

Glossary

astronaut: a person who is trained to work in space

crew: the people working on a ship or space station

data: information

International Space Station: a science lab that circles Earth. People live on it. Sixteen countries helped design it.

laser: a narrow beam of light

probe: a robot that explores outer space

rover: a vehicle that drives across planets

sensor: a part of a robot that lets it understand its environment

solar system: the sun, along with the asteroids, comets, moons, and planets that circle around it

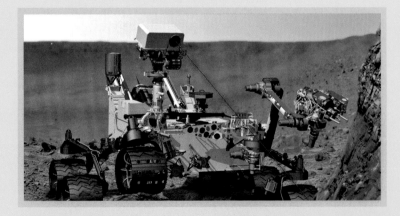

Further Reading

Canadian Space Agency:
Meet Dextre
http://www.asc-csa.gc.ca/eng/iss/dextre/profile.asp

Hamilton, S. L. *Robots and Rovers.* Edina, MN:
Abdo Publishing, 2011.

Kops, Deborah. *Exploring Space Robots.*
Minneapolis: Lerner Publications, 2012.

NASA: *Cassini*
http://saturn.jpl.nasa.gov/kids

NASA: *Curiosity* Rover
http://mars.jpl.nasa.gov/msl/mission/rover

NASA Education: *Robot Storybook*
http://www.nasa.gov/audience/forstudents/k-4
/stories/ames-robot-storybook-text.html

Parker, Steve. *Robots in Space.* Mankato, MN:
Amicus, 2011.

Index

Photo Acknowledgments

The images in this book are used with the permission of: NASA, pp. 2, 5, 6, 7, 8, 10, 11, 12, 13, 14, 15, 16, 17, 18, 19, 20, 21, 22, 24, 25, 26, 27, 28, 30, 31; © Stavchansky Yakov /Shutterstock Images, p. 4; © Ryan Wick/Flickr, p. 9; © Damian Dovarganes/AP Images, p. 23.

Front Cover: Courtesy of NASA (Curiosity Rover) and NASA/JPL-Caltech/University of Arizona (Earth and moon).

Main body text set in Johann Light 30/36.